CATS

SIAMESE CATS

by Elizabeth Andrews

Cody Koala
An Imprint of Pop!
popbooksonline.com

Hello! My name is Cody Koala

This book is filled with videos, puzzles, games, and more! Scan the QR codes* while you read, or visit the website below to make this book pop.

popbooksonline.com/siamese

*Scanning QR codes requires a web-enabled smart device with a QR code reader app and a camera.

abdobooks.com

Published by Pop!, a division of ABDO, PO Box 398166, Minneapolis, Minnesota 55439.

Printed in the United States of America, North Mankato, Minnesota.

102022
012023

THIS BOOK CONTAINS RECYCLED MATERIALS

Cover Photo: Shutterstock Images
Interior Photos: Shutterstock Images; Alamy Images
Editor: Grace Hansen
Series Designer: Colleen McLaren

Library of Congress Control Number: 2022941110

Publisher's Cataloging-in-Publication Data
Names: Andrews, Elizabeth, author.
Title: Siamese cats / by Elizabeth Andrews
Description: Minneapolis, Minnesota : Pop!, 2023 | Series: Cats | Includes online resources and index.
Identifiers: ISBN 9781098243159 (lib. bdg.) | ISBN 9781098243852 (ebook)
Subjects: LCSH: Siamese cat--Juvenile literature. | Cat, Domestic--Juvenile literature. | Shorthair cat--Juvenile literature. | Zoology--Juvenile literature.
Classification: DDC 636.825--dc23

Table of Contents

Chapter 1
Feline Royalty 4

Chapter 2
Chatty Cats 10

Chapter 3
Cat Care. 14

Chapter 4
Kittens 18

Making Connections 22
Glossary 23
Index. 24
Online Resources 24

Chapter 1

Feline Royalty

Siamese cats are one of the oldest cat **breeds**. They **originated** in Siam which is the country now called Thailand. They guarded Siam's palaces and **temples**.

Watch a video here!

Siamese cats have an **elegant** look. Their bodies are long and slim with thin

bones. But they are strong. Their blue eyes are large and almond shaped.

chocolate

lilac

seal

blue

Siamese cats have a short, smooth, pointed coat. This means they have darker fur on their large ears, face, legs, and tail. Their bodies are cream or white. Their points are **seal**, blue, chocolate, or lilac.

Dark points occur on parts of the cat's body that get the coldest.

Chapter 2

Chatty Cats

Siamese cats are very smart. It is easy to play with them and teach them tricks. They get along with other animals. These cats have a deep meow that they use all the time.

There are up to 21 different sounds cats can use to communicate! Siamese cats are one of the most talkative **breeds**.

Learn more here!

Siamese cats are loving and want to be near their family. They are known to choose a favorite family member. The cats enjoy curling up on a lap or even on a book their owner is reading.

Chapter 3

Cat Care

Siamese cats are very social. They do not like being ignored and will meow when they need attention. It may be helpful to get another cat for them to play with.

Explore links here!

Siamese cats spend much of their day cleaning themselves with their scratchy tongues. Fresh

water and food should always be available. They need their **litter boxes** cleaned daily.

Chapter 4

Kittens

Siamese kittens are born completely white or cream in color. The dark points they are known for will begin to show as they grow.

Complete an activity here!

Siamese cats often have **litters** of four to six kittens. Kittens stay with their mother for 12 to 16 weeks. Then they are ready to go to their new homes!

Making Connections

Text-to-Self

Do you think you would like a talkative cat? Explain why or why not.

Text-to-Text

Have you read any other books about a cat from a specific place or country? How was it similar to or different from the Siamese cat?

Text-to-World

What other kinds of animals were known to protect important people or places?

Glossary

breed – a particular type or kind of animal.

elegant – fine, graceful, and lovely.

litter– all kittens born at one time to a mother cat.

litter box – a box filled with cat litter, which is like sand. Cats use litter boxes to bury their waste.

originated – began to exist; produced or created.

seal – brown in color with a reddish undertone in certain light.

temple – a building or place where a god or gods are worshiped.

Index

body, 6–7

care, 14, 16–17

coat, 8–9

coloring, 8, 18

eyes, 7

food, 17

grooming, 16

kittens, 18, 21

noises, 10, 14

personality, 10, 13–14

Siam (Thailand), 4

Online Resources

popbooksonline.com

Thanks for reading this Cody Koala book!

This book is filled with videos, puzzles, games, and more! Scan the QR codes* while you read, or visit the website below to make this book pop.

popbooksonline.com/siamese

*Scanning QR codes requires a web-enabled smart device with a QR code reader app and a camera.